Virtue Seeds

ACTIVITIES TO EXPLORE VIRTUES

By Elaheh Bos

www.plantlovegrow.com
©Plantlovegrow 2016
©Elaheh Bos 2016

ISBN: 978-0-9810556-3-3

Legal Deposit, Library and Archives
Canada, 2016

Table of Contents

plant
love
grow

How to use the Virtue Activity Guide

This guide was created as a tool to help teach virtues through group activities, discussions and games. These activities provide learning and discussion opportunities between parents, children, and educators.

Quotes:

Special space has been provided for inspirational quotes. These can be religious, spiritual, scientific, or beautiful sayings that you create to focus your energy on the virtue you are exploring. These quotes can be memorized and are there to provide inspiration.

What you need in your tool box:

- Paper towels.
- Glue (appropriate to age, glue stick is often the easiest).
- Craft paper, magazines, recycled paper, white papers for drawing.
- Scissors (age appropriate).
- Pencil, crayons or markers (what I call colouring or drawing tools).
- Paint and paintbrushes.
- A box full of things you would normally recycle.
- Copies of the activity and colouring pages (enough for everyone).

We suggest giving each child a binder for them to keep their finished projects or to write about the activities. Ask them to personalize their binders.

Before starting any activity:

1. Discuss together three to five simple guidelines for the group to follow during the activities. These guidelines should be inspired by virtues and should focus on the desired behaviour.

2. Preparation is key. Choose the activity ahead of time and prepare your materials. Prepare your space. If you plan on using the virtue guide as part of a scheduled class, read all the activities ahead and add them to your calendar. Always make extra copies of the material you plan to use.

3. Create a routine around the activities. If you do them on a daily basis, arrange a specific time each day. If you do them on a weekly basis, do them on the same day if possible. Everyone will begin to anticipate the next activity with excitement.

4. Create roles and responsibilities to match the age of the children. This will be a great opportunity for them to learn responsibility, and will allow everyone to be involved and feel responsible for the success of the activity.

5. Focus on the process, not the outcome. Learning, spending time together, discussing what a virtue means to us, sharing our own stories and trying something new is more important than the results of an activity. Enjoy the process and discussions.

1. Caring

Understanding Caring:

Here are some words associated with Caring.

| THOUGHTFUL | COMPASSIONATE |

| GENTLE | CONSIDERATE | HELPFUL |

Using 2 of them, write your own definition of what Caring means to you.

_____

_____

OR

Write 2 sentences showing people practicing Caring using 1 suggested word in each sentence.

_____

_____

A beautiful quote about Caring:

Write down a quote that you wish to memorize or remember.
If you cannot find a quote to inspire you, try coming up with your own.

Activity 1: Comic strip on caring

Create a one page comic strip with a short story about caring. Work alone or in groups to come up with your characters and your story line. Here are some steps to help you in the process.

1. Have scrap paper ready to practice and try out different things. Give yourself time to try different ideas.
2. Think about who or what your concept is going to be about. Caring can be interpreted in many different ways and can be used in many different kind of scenarios.
3. When you have an idea of what you want to do, write a title.
4. Decide who your main character is going to be (person, animal, stick man etc.)
5. Draw different boxes in which your cartoon will appear or use the sample on page 41.
6. Add some humour if you can.
7. Focus on your story. Make it simple or complex.
8. Don't worry about making your comic too detailed. Create simple characters and don't forget the theme.

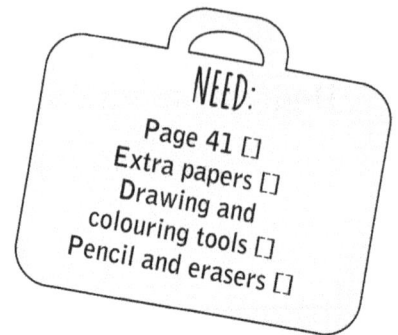

HAVE FUN!

Activity 2: Caring words

NEED:
Writing tools []
Papers []

Write a Haiku on the topic of caring.

A Haiku is a short poem written in a very specific way.
A Haiku has only 3 lines.
The first line has 5 syllables,
the second has 7 syllables,
and the last one has 5 syllables.

Haiku poems often use nature as a metaphor, but feel free to be creative. After you have written your Haiku about caring, share it with someone, or if you wish, write more than one. Writing a Haiku is not an easy task and if you are having trouble, don't give up. Be creative and try writing a different kind of poem instead.

Virtue Challenge: A two minute project.

Ask someone how they are doing and listen and care about their answer.

WILL TRY   DONE

2. Cooperation

Understanding Cooperation:

Here are some words associated with Cooperation.

> COLLABORATION   ASSISTANCE
>
> TEAMWORK   MUTUAL AID   JOIN

Using 2 of them, write your own definition of what Cooperation means to you.

_____

_____

OR

Write 2 sentences showing people practicing Cooperation using 1 suggested word in each sentence.

_____

_____

A beautiful quote about Cooperation:
Write down a quote that you wish to memorize or remember.
If you cannot find a quote to inspire you, try coming up with your own.

Activity 1: Toothpick Project

Create a unique artwork by cooperating in a very specific way. For your first project, have each person take a turn placing and taping or gluing down their toothpick on the large paper or cardboard. No one should know what the other person is doing and what the final image will look like. There should be no directives given as to the type of drawing or art created. Let each person choose how they want to place their toothpick. When finished, look at your picture and discuss how the process took place. Discuss how it felt to cooperate without being given any directions.

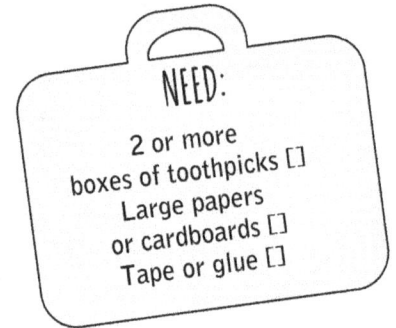

NEED:
2 or more boxes of toothpicks []
Large papers or cardboards []
Tape or glue []

For your second project, decide in advance what you plan on achieving and how everyone is going to cooperate. Discuss the results and differences between the two projects.

Activity 2: A unique orchestra

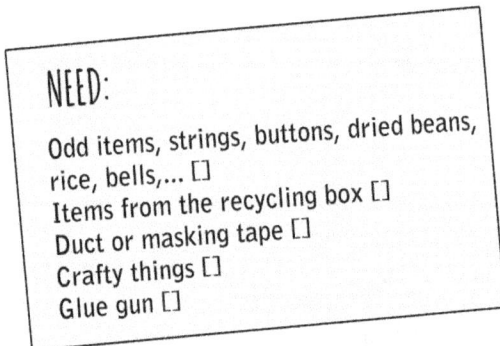

NEED:
Odd items, strings, buttons, dried beans, rice, bells,... []
Items from the recycling box []
Duct or masking tape []
Crafty things []
Glue gun []

The goal of this activity is to create one unique orchestra by combining many different sounds and instruments. Have each person create an instrument from the items provided. Have them present their instrument to the group. Collaborate together in smaller teams or as one big group to create an orchestra from all these unique instruments. Discuss how it felt to cooperate together.

Virtue Challenge: A lifetime project.

Think of the virtues and skills you need to cooperate with others.
Ask yourself these questions:
Am I a good listener?
Do I let others participate?
Am I patient with others?
Do I think my ideas are always better?
Think of your answers and what virtues you can practice
to become better at cooperating with others.

WILL TRY   DONE

3. Compassion

Understanding Compassion:

Here are some words associated with Compassion.

SYMPATHY   CARE

EMPATHY   CONCERN   CONSIDERATION

Using 2 of them, write your own definition of what Compassion means to you.

_____

_____

OR

Write 2 sentences showing people practicing Compassion using 1 suggested word in each sentence.

_____

_____

A beautiful quote about Compassion:
Write down a quote that you wish to
memorize or remember. If you cannot
find a quote to inspire you, try coming
up with your own.

Activity 1: Looking beyond stereotypes

Discuss what stereotypes are. If you don't know the word, look it up in a dictionary. Think about what happens when we believe stereotypes or when we create them. What happens when we make assumptions about others? Talk about different stereotypes or which stereotypes are sometimes associated with different people.
What is the stereotype associated with a homeless person?
Someone in a wheelchair? A politician? Someone with a contagious disease?
A rich person? A person in prison? A movie star? A professional athlete? A teacher?
A police officer? A housewife An accountant?

NEED:
Labels []
Papers []
Pens []

Discuss why stereotypes create problems and limit us from really getting to know people. Think of different characteristics each of these people could have that would defy the stereotypes associated with them. Discuss these as well.

Take a couple of labels and write different stereotypes that people might use to define you. Stick the labels on yourself. Look at each label and decide if they define you. If not, why not? If they don't define you, take them off. What can you conclude about stereotypes? How does compassion allow us to look beyond stereotypes?

Activity 2: Imagine

Read the scenarios given in the first column on page 43 and try to imagine what is going on in the life of that person leading them to do what they are currently doing. Think of different possible scenarios. Write what could possibly be happening for each of the people in the scenarios. Share your answers with each other and discuss how we can be more compassionate towards others. In each of these scenarios, what could you have assumed instead? How does compassion help us?

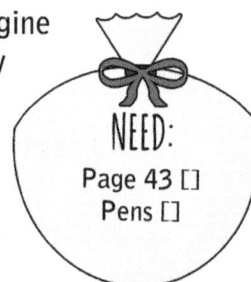

NEED:
Page 43 []
Pens []

Virtue Challenge: Changing your frame of mind.

Whenever you are about to make an assumption about something, ask yourself:

WHAT ELSE COULD BE HAPPENING?

WHAT WOULD I DO IF I WERE IN THEIR SHOES?

WILL TRY   DONE

4. Determination

Understanding Determination:

Here are some words associated with Determination.

STRENGTH   WILLPOWER

RESOLVE   PERSEVERANCE   ENDURANCE

Using 2 of them, write your own definition of what Determination means to you.

_____

_____

OR

Write 2 sentences showing people practicing Determination using 1 suggested word in each sentence.

_____

_____

A beautiful quote about Determination:
Write down a quote that you wish to memorize or remember.
If you cannot find a quote to inspire you, try coming up with your own.

Activity 1: I am a possibility

On a poster or a large paper, write these words in big letters:

I am a possibility.

Around those words, write or draw things that you might possibly do, places that you could possibly visit, things that you would want to accomplish, or anything else that you feel should be on your possibility poster. Write down quotes that inspire you to be determined and things that you have already accomplished and are proud of. Share your posters and discuss how determination affects our possibilities.

Activity 2: Map Quest

On the bottom left hand corner of the sheet, write down a problem that requires a lot of determination to be resolved. It can be an actual challenge you face, or something you make up. On the right side of the sheet, write down different possible outcomes. Have some of them show possible solutions while others lead to dead ends or more complications. Create a map that leads you from the problem to the solution. Make sure to include all the challenges you could possibly face along the way, as well as the strengths and virtues you call upon to finish your journey. Create different routes and look for possible ways to get to where you want to go. Be creative when making your map and have fun with it.

Think about your map as a metaphor for your life.
What can you learn from your journey?

How does determination impact your journey?

Virtue Challenge: A three month project.

Think about the role that determination plays in learning to save money.
Make it your goal to save a certain amount per month or week.
Keep doing this for three months and see what happens.
After three months, do not spend that money.
Instead use the habit you have learned to keep going for another three months.
Keep doing it three months at a time.

WILL TRY   DONE

5. Forgiveness

Understanding Forgiveness:

Here are some words associated with Forgiveness.

PARDON   MERCY

UNDERSTANDING   COMPASSION   KINDNESS

Using 2 of them, write your own definition of what Forgiveness means to you.

_____

_____

OR

Write 2 sentences showing people practicing Forgiveness using 1 suggested word in each sentence.

_____

_____

A beautiful quote about Forgiveness:
Write down a quote that you wish to memorize or remember.
If you cannot find a quote to inspire you, try coming up with your own.

Activity 1: Everybody makes mistakes

Sometimes forgiving someone can be hard, but it helps to remember that everybody makes mistakes. Discuss how we make mistakes too, but that doesn't mean that we are bad people.
Write down three mistakes that you have made in the past.
Next to that write down what you wish you had done instead.
Write the words: "I forgive myself" on the top of your paper and forgive yourself for these mistakes. Write something that will inspire you to forgive others. It should be simple and short and can mention the reasons why we should forgive others and the consequences to ourselves if you do not.

NEED:
Writing tools []
Papers []

I forgive
myself

Activity 2: Forgiveness debate

Come up with a scenario in which one person must forgive someone else. Make two teams if possible and have each team come up with as many different points to debate FOR or AGAINST forgiving someone who has done something. Make several scenarios if necessary so that each team gets a turn at arguing both sides.

If you do not have enough people, argue both sides of the issue.

What are your conclusions?

Discuss how forgiveness affects us emotionally, mentally, physically or spiritually.

NEED:
Writing tools []
Papers []

Virtue Challenge: A ten minute project.

Think about something that happened a long time ago that you are still holding on to.
Maybe you haven't quite forgiven someone else or yourself for making a mistake.
Write down the following words with an open heart:
I am open to forgiving...
I am open to letting go of...
I will happily let go of ... and welcome (write what you want to welcome instead) into my life.

Now that I have forgiven ... I am free!

WILL TRY   DONE

6. Generosity

Understanding Generosity:

Here are some words associated with Generosity.

> BIG HEART   CHARITY

> KINDNESS   ASSISTANCE   COMPASSION

Using 2 of them, write your own definition of what Generosity means to you.

_____

_____

OR

Write 2 sentences showing people practicing Generosity using 1 suggested word in each sentence.

_____

_____

A beautiful quote about Generosity:

Write down a quote that you wish to memorize or remember.
If you cannot find a quote to inspire you, try coming up with your own.

Activity 1: Make a sharing box

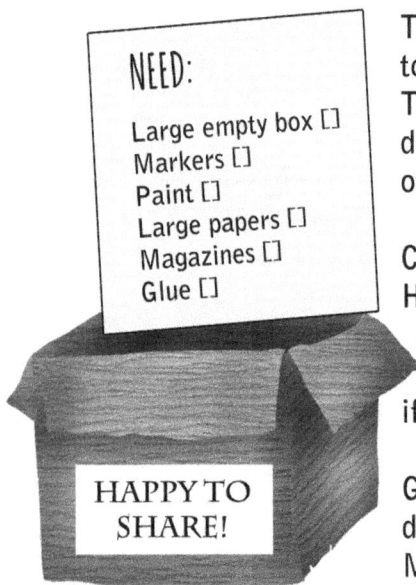

NEED:

Large empty box []
Markers []
Paint []
Large papers []
Magazines []
Glue []

HAPPY TO SHARE!

Think of how fortunate you are and make a list of what you are grateful to have in your life. Think of others who may be less fortunate. To make your sharing box, decorate a large box with different images, drawings, and words. Be creative. Try writing things that can inspire others to be generous too. Write that this is a sharing box.

Create your own rules about how your sharing box will be used. Here is one idea: a sharing box is a box where everyone can put in something that they don't use or need so it can be shared with other people. Explain that everyone can take what they need, use it, keep it if they need or bring it back when they are done.

Go through your things and place whatever you are willing to share or donate into the sharing box. Encourage your friends to do the same. Make as many sharing boxes as you can and place them where they can be of use to others.

As you are making the boxes, discuss what society teaches us about being generous, about having everything for ourselves, about consuming and materialism.

Activity 2: Share a gift that means something to you

NEED:
Colouring tools []
Writing tools []
Papers []

Discuss the concept of giving gifts and talk about different gifts you have received and given over time. Discuss how sometimes we focus so much on what the gift is that we forget to fully appreciate that generosity is not about what you give. Have you ever given a gift that did not cost anything? Why not? Go through your things and either find something that you are willing to share or make something. Think about your mind, your heart and your hands as the only instruments that can create amazing gifts. On a sheet of paper make a list of possible gifts you can make or things you can share with others. Make one of those gifts now and write a card (by folding the paper in two) explaining why this gift is special to you and how you hope it will be special to the person you will be sharing it with. Remember that the important thing is to be creative and sincere. Give the gift you made and remember you do not need a reason to be generous. Keep your list handy for the future.

Virtue Challenge: A two minute project.
Share something you love with someone else.

WILL TRY   DONE

---

7. Helpfulness

Understanding Helpfulness:

Here are some words associated with Helpfulness.

CONCERN   CARE

ASSISTANCE   SUPPORT   USEFULNESS

Using 2 of them, write your own definition of what Helpfulness means to you.

_____

_____

OR

Write 2 sentences showing people practicing Helpfulness using 1 suggested word in each sentence.

_____

_____

A beautiful quote about Helpfulness:
Write down a quote that you wish to memorize or remember.
If you cannot find a quote to inspire you, try coming up with your own.

Activity 1: A few words

We sometimes take for granted how much work goes into learning a new language. A nice way to be helpful is to make the effort of learning a few words in a new language. Think of how great it could be to surprise someone by saying hello, thank you, or other words in their language.

NEED:
Page 45 []
Writing tools []
Papers []

Look at page 45. Here are a few languages to start with. Learn the words you can and do some research to find other words in different languages. Find out what languages are spoken in your neighborhood or your school and those spoken by your friends. Add as many languages as you can. Research what are the top ten spoken languages in the world. Wouldn't it be nice to be able to say a few words in all of them? Discuss how making an effort to learn someone else's language is a way of practicing helpfulness.

Hello!

Au revoir

Activity 2: Helping hands

NEED:
An hour of your time []
Willingness to help []
Paintbrushes []
Papers []
Pens []
Paint []

Imagine that your hands could only be used for helping. Describe what it would mean to have helping hands. What would the world be like if everyone had helping hands? Write a poem, story, or describe what a world filled with helping hands would look like. Next to what you have written, make a handprint of both your hands as a symbol that you too can have helping hands whenever you choose. Take an hour out of your day and for that hour act with helping hands. What can you do with your helping hands?

Virtue Challenge: A monthly challenge.

Find out if you can volunteer at a hospital, a home for the elderly,
a community center or anywhere you feel you can help.
Make sure you get permission from your parents first.
Talk to the people who operate the place and offer one afternoon per month to start.
It doesn't matter what you end up doing,
just think of what you are adding to other people's lives
by being there.

WILL TRY   DONE

8. Honesty

Understanding Honesty:

Here are some words associated with Honesty.

| SINCERITY | TRUTHFULNESS |

| INTEGRITY | FRANKNESS | OPENNESS |

Using 2 of them, write your own definition of what Honesty means to you.

_____

_____

OR

Write 2 sentences showing people practicing Honesty using 1 suggested word in each sentence.

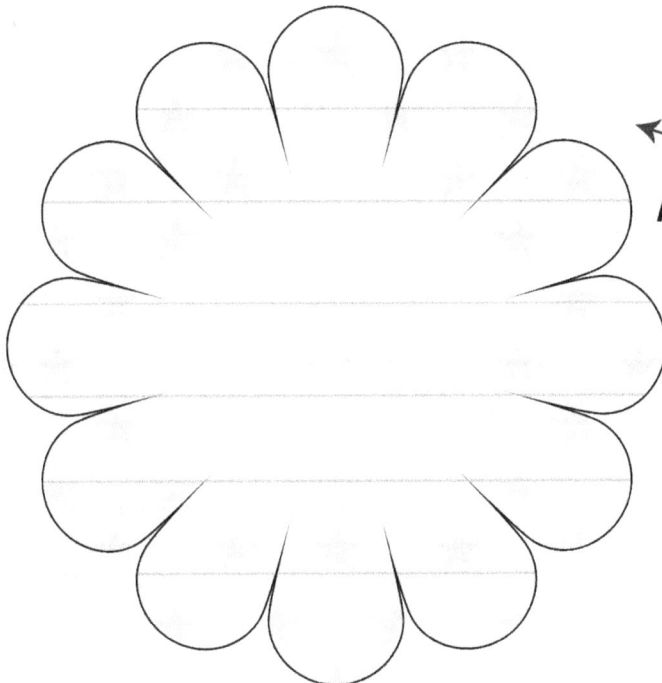

_____

_____

A beautiful quote about Honesty:

Write down a quote that you wish
to memorize or remember.
If you cannot find a quote to inspire you,
try coming up with your own.

Activity 1: My coat of arms

The coat of arms dates back to the 12th Century in Europe. During this period a woven cloth would be placed over the armor of knights and soldiers to establish their identity. These images would often be accompanied with a short sentence explaining the values the person or family lived by. A family's coat of arms would identify the family as well as provide a mark of pride that the family could live by. Imagine that you are the descendent of a family renowned for their honesty, sincerity, truthfulness and courage. Look at page 47 and complete your family's coat of arms. Make sure to write a sentence to go with it sharing how honesty is part of your virtues.

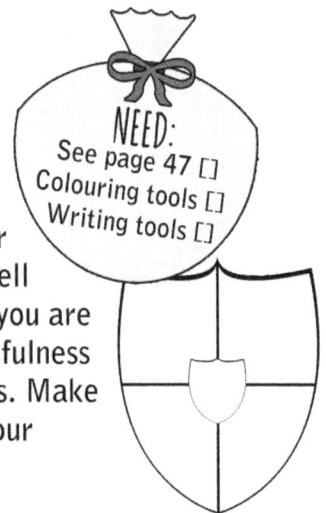

NEED:
See page 47 []
Colouring tools []
Writing tools []

Think of a family legend that might have come down through the years showing honesty and write it down. Maybe part of this legend can be illustrated in your coat of arms.

Activity 2: Truth Compass

*Page 49 should be photocopied on card stock or thick paper
*For securing multiple sheets of paper together, allowing for the rotation of the needles.

NEED:

Page 49* []
Scissors []
Glue []
Brass fastener
(split pins)* []

Discuss how sometimes in order to avoid the consequences of our actions, it is easier to lie than to tell the truth. Write down at least 5 reasons why it is important to tell the truth and make yourself a truth compass by following these directions.

Cut the compass from your copy of page 49. Make sure to cut out the 2 needles or make your own needles. In the inner circle of the compass, write a sentence reminding you of the importance of telling the truth. In the other sections, write reminders of things you can do to help you practice honesty. Use the brass fastener to assemble the needles on the compass. Colour it or decorate it and place the compass somewhere where it can remind you of the importance of telling the truth.

Virtue Challenge: Changing habits.

Think of how many little white lies we tell others and ourselves.
Make a commitment to be more honest with yourself and those you care about.
Develop the habit of thinking about what you say and understand the power of your words.
Be polite, tactful and remember that sometimes the best answer is to say nothing at all.

WILL TRY   DONE

---

9. Joyfulness

Understanding Joyfulness:

Here are some words associated with Joyfulness.

PLEASURE	CHEERFUL

HAPPINESS	ENJOYMENT	DELIGHT

Using 2 of them, write your own definition of what Joyfulness means to you.

_____

_____

OR

Write 2 sentences showing people practicing Joyfulness using 1 suggested word in each sentence.

_____

_____

A beautiful quote about Joyfulness:

Write down a quote that you wish
to memorize or remember.
If you cannot find a quote to inspire you,
try coming up with your own.

Activity 1: Catalogue of joyfulness

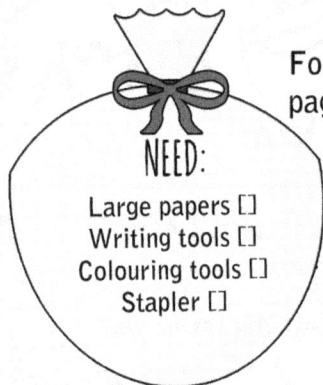

Fold 3 to 4 large sheets of paper in 2 to make a catalogue of about 6 to 8 pages. Staple your pages together as if you are making a book. Imagine that it is your job to create a catalogue of joyfulness. What would this catalogue look like? Draw and write about the different types of activities and things that bring joy. Have fun!
Here are some suggestions for your catalogue:

• Create a front and back.

• Use categories such as morning joyfulness, joyful outdoor moments...

• Add a table of content if you want to have many categories.

• Don't forget that this is your catalogue. You decide what it should look like.

Activity 2: Gratitude box

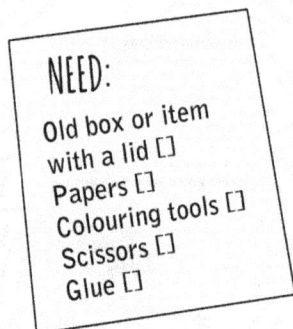

Close your eyes and think about the people in your life, the experiences you have had, the things you have done and the places you have been to. Think about the virtues, qualities and gifts that you have, the talents and the abilities you have been given and have been working on. Look at the box as a symbol of yourself - your inner self and your outer self. Decorate the outside of the box in a way that represents you. Once you have decorated the outside of the box, write down what qualities or virtues that you have within you and are grateful for. You may list people, experiences, things or events.

Share the outside of your box with others but what you put inside the box is only for you. Discuss what gratitude teaches us about joyfulness?

Virtue Challenge: A whole day project.

Think of a child in your family (brother, sister, cousin, friend)
and spend a day with them doing only fun things.
Let them choose the activity and make sure to participate fully.

WILL TRY   DONE

---

10. Justice

Understanding Justice:

Here are some words associated with Justice.

| FAIRNESS | EQUALITY |
| PEACE | HONESTY | INTEGRITY |

Using 2 of them, write your own definition of what Justice means to you.

_____

_____

OR

Write 2 sentences showing people practicing Justice using 1 suggested word in each sentence.

_____

_____

A beautiful quote about Justice:

Write down a quote that you wish to memorize or remember.
If you cannot find a quote to inspire you, try coming up with your own.

Activity 1: Justice Superhero

Think about what superheroes do. What do they fight for?
Who do they fight against? Create a superhero who would fight
for justice. What would he or she look like? Draw that superhero.
What is his/her name? What are his/her powers?
Share your superhero with others and share 3 qualities you
have in common with your justice superhero.
Discuss whether or not you have to have powers to fight
for justice? What can each of us do?

NEED:
Colouring tools []
Drawing tools []
Papers []

Activity 2: Name the consequences

Discuss what consequences are and why we need consequences. What would happen if
we lived in a world with no consequences? Discuss whether positive consequences have
the same effect as negative consequences.
Think of everything you have done today and write down 5 things
you did that led to positive consequences and 5 things you did
that led to negative consequences. What could you have done
differently? Share what you have written and discuss whether
the idea of consequences influenced your actions and if so,
why or why not?

NEED:
Writing tools []
Papers []

Virtue Challenge: One thing to help.

Look at the world around you. There are many different kinds of injustices. Extreme wealth and
poverty is just one example. Think of one thing you can do to help a stranger - just one thing.
You may think it's not much, but it can make a huge difference if you actually follow through
with your idea. Think of something you can donate, a place where you can volunteer,
or whatever is within your possibilities.

You can always make a difference.
Don't worry how big or how small your deed may seem.
A little goes a long way!

WILL TRY   DONE

11. Kindness

Understanding Kindness:

Here are some words associated with Kindness.

COMPASSION   SYMPATHY

BIG HEART   CONSIDERATE   HELPFUL

Using 2 of them, write your own definition of what Kindness means to you.

_____

_____

OR

Write 2 sentences showing people practicing Kindness using 1 suggested word in each sentence.

_____

_____

A beautiful quote about Kindness:
Write down a quote that you wish to memorize or remember.
If you cannot find a quote to inspire you, try coming up with your own.

Activity 1: Before and after

NEED:
Writing tools []
Papers []

Discuss how a simple act of kindness can really help someone. Pretend that you are making a television show and that you are the producer in charge. Create a **before and after** type of show.
Write down the title of your program, who will be the person helped on the show and how they will be helped. Will it be a surprise or will they know? Have fun thinking of many different possibilities and scenarios.

Assign different roles and act them out. Share your television show with others. What acts of kindness you can do for someone around you? Can you actually make your show a reality for someone you know?

Activity 2: Creating a commercial

Discuss the impact of commercials on our society and how effective commercials can influence what we buy and what we do. Share your favourite commercials. What do they sell? How long do they run? How much do you think they cost to produce?

NEED:
Writing tools []
Drawing tools []
Papers []

Now team up to create a commercial to promote kindness.
Come up with the concept and ideas and write the script for your commercial.

Draw or sketch the visual elements. If you feel inspired, see if you can act it out and tape it.

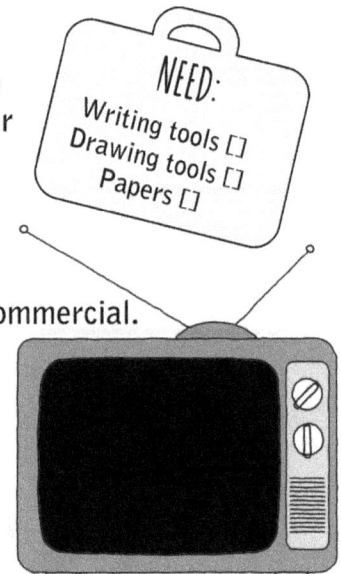

Virtue Challenge: Kindness Patrol.

Create a Kindness Patrol in your school. Create little cards that say something like (make up your own text): We have caught you doing something kind. You should be proud of yourself for being a good example. Thank you.
Sign it as "The Kindness Patrol." Get permission from your teachers, get your friends involved and monitor your school for a week handing out your kindness acknowledgement slips. What do you notice after a week?

Decide if it is worth continuing.

WILL TRY   DONE

12. Moderation

Understanding Moderation:

Here are some words associated with Moderation.

SELF-CONTROL   SELF RESPECT

CHOICES   BALANCE   DISCIPLINE

Using 2 of them, write your own definition of what Moderation means to you.

_____

_____

OR

Write 2 sentences showing people practicing Moderation using 1 suggested word in each sentence.

_____

_____

A beautiful quote about Moderation: Write down a quote that you wish to memorize or remember. If you cannot find a quote to inspire you, try coming up with your own.

Activity 1: What tune are you listening to?

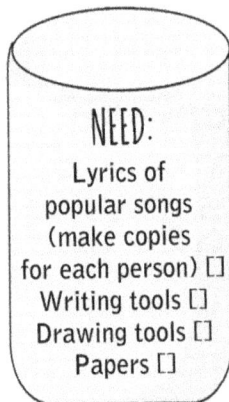

NEED:
Lyrics of popular songs (make copies for each person) []
Writing tools []
Drawing tools []
Papers []

Discuss what moderation means to you and if we should strive to have moderation in all things. What are your thoughts about moderation in music? Is it possible? Can you actually have moderation when it comes to the arts? Imagine that you have a radio that can produce two different kinds of music. Draw your radio on your paper and have music coming out from each side. On one station you have music that is unfiltered, and on the other you have more moderate music. What would moderate music sound like?
Either individually or in groups, rewrite some sections of popular music to fit the new moderate station if it's necessary.

Activity 2: Movie Messages

Watch and discuss a movie together.
Use the following questions as a guideline for your discussion:

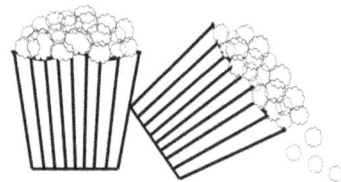

What messages did this movie send about being moderate in our choices?
What messages did this movie send about being overly materialistic?
What other messages were conveyed in the movie?
If you could add something to the movie, what would it be?
If you could change something in the movie, what would it be?
What messages does this movie send?
Who is the target audience for this movie?

If you could change the movie (with the goal of changing the message) what would you change?

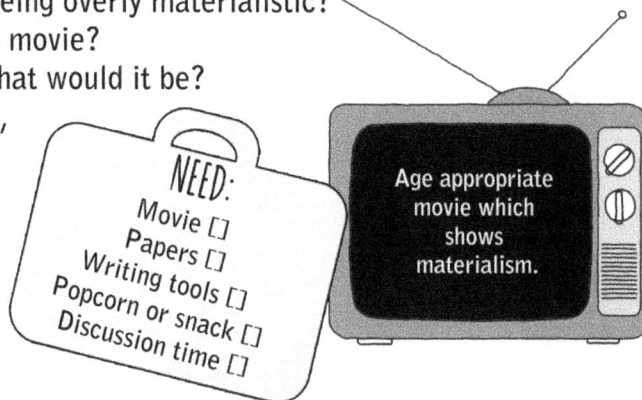

NEED:
Movie []
Papers []
Writing tools []
Popcorn or snack []
Discussion time []

Age appropriate movie which shows materialism.

Virtue Challenge: An afternoon project.

Do you have a local food bank?
Look inside your cupboard and see if you have some things that you can share.
Get your friends to do the same.
Collect some cash and buy food to donate.
Canned food and non-perishables are usually the best things to donate.

Ask yourself: Can I do more?

WILL TRY   DONE

13. Modesty

Understanding Modesty:

Here are some words associated with Modesty.

HUMILITY   UNPRETENTIOUS

APPROPRIATE   CONSIDERATE   RESPECTFUL

Using 2 of them, write your own definition of what Modesty means to you.

_____

_____

OR

Write 2 sentences showing people practicing Modesty using 1 suggested word in each sentence.

_____

_____

A beautiful quote about Modesty:

Write down a quote that you wish to memorize or remember.
If you cannot find a quote to inspire you, try coming up with your own.

Activity 1: How we used to dress

Discuss how people used to dress in the past and how people dress now. Pick a time in history or a culture that you would like to explore and research how people used to dress at that time or in that area. Make a list of things that influence fashion or cause it to be different from one place to the next.

NEED:
Trip to the library or access to internet []
Writing tools []
Papers []

Compare what people used to wear then to what people are wearing now. Discuss who should assume more responsibility for the messages that different fashion trends convey. Is this the role of companies or the consumer? What would responsible fashion look like? Imagine that you had to create your own fashion label. What would it stand for? Write the mission statement for your label (a few sentences that define what your fashion label represents) and give the reason behind it as well as its overall goal and vision. Discuss how modesty is connected to how we perceive others and ourselves.

Activity 2: My magazine – my message

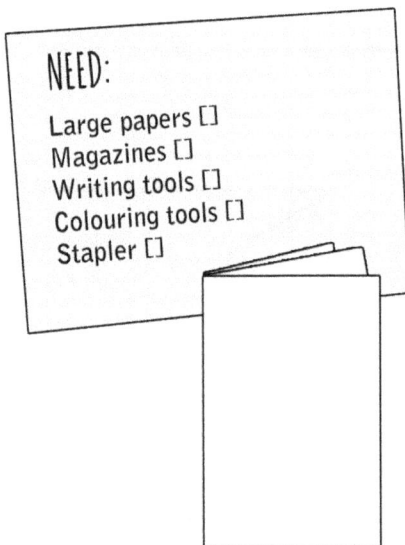

NEED:
Large papers []
Magazines []
Writing tools []
Colouring tools []
Stapler []

Write your definition of modesty. Discuss whether you feel modesty still has a place in this time. Look through a fashion or magazine and read a couple of articles. With a marker, circle everything that DOES NOT show a good example of modesty.

Now create your own magazine with your own message. Decide what you want your magazine to say and put your message inside.

Fold 3-4 large sheets of paper in 2 and use images, drawings and text to create your own magazine of about 6 to 8 pages. Talk about what messages are targeted at your age group in today's society and what you can do to send another message out there. Feel free to explore various topics and try running a small edition to share with others. Do you think your magazine would sell as well as others? Why or why not?

Virtue Challenge: A half an hour project.

Go through your clothes. What do they say about you?

☐ ☐
WILL TRY   DONE

---

14. Obedience

Understanding Obedience:

Here are some words associated with Obedience.

| AGREEMENT | OBSERVANCE |
| RESPECT | DUTY | LOYALTY |

Using 2 of them, write your own definition of what Obedience means to you.

_____

_____

OR

Write 2 sentences showing people practicing Obedience using 1 suggested word in each sentence.

_____

_____

A beautiful quote about Obedience:
Write down a quote that you wish
to memorize or remember.
If you cannot find a quote to inspire you,
try coming up with your own.

Activity 1: A better society

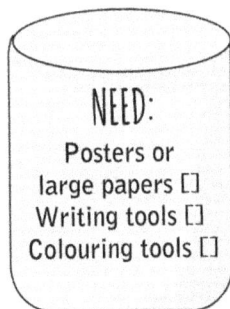

NEED:

Posters or
large papers []
Writing tools []
Colouring tools []

Think of the world at large. What are some of the laws and rules in place that ensure a better society for everyone. Talk about laws or guidelines that should be in place, but may not yet be. Think about rules that would ensure the survival of everyone. Should we have rules for peace in the world? Rules for the environment? Rules to make sure everyone has enough? Create a poster showing what laws would be necessary to create a better society. Discuss if you feel virtues should be guidelines for a better world?

Share your poster with others.

Activity 2: To obey or not to obey

NEED:

Writing tools []
Papers []

Think of different situations in which you are asked to obey certain rules or guidelines. These can be within your home, within your social circle or as a member of society. On a piece of paper make two columns. In the right column write **REASONS TO OBEY**, in the left column write **REASONS NOT TO OBEY**. Fill in the column with as many examples as you can think of. Discuss the main reasons behind rules and laws and whether it is better to obey or not and under what circumstances.

Discuss free choice and what should be done when one person's choice affects someone else's ability to choose.

Virtue Challenge: An anytime project.

Do you find yourself being asked to do something over and over again?
Surprise someone by doing something without being asked.
It doesn't matter what you do, just do it with the right intention and the right attitude.

How does it feel to surprise someone by being obedient even before being asked?
What was the other person's reaction?
Is it worth doing again?

WILL TRY   DONE

15. Patience

Understanding Patience:

Here are some words associated with Patience.

DETERMINATION   PERSISTENCE

ENDURANCE   PERSEVERANCE   FORTITUDE

Using 2 of them, write your own definition of what Patience means to you.

_____

_____

OR

Write 2 sentences showing people practicing Patience using 1 suggested word in each sentence.

_____

_____

A beautiful quote about Patience:

Write down a quote that you wish
to memorize or remember.
If you cannot find a quote to inspire you,
try coming up with your own.

Activity 1: My patient side

NEED:
Large papers or poster []
Drawing tools []
Colouring tools []
Scissors []
Tape []

Discuss how being patient is an important part of life. Discuss how you practice patience. Tape several papers together to create one large paper or use a poster. Lie down and have someone else trace your outline. Help each other in the process.

Once you have the outline, trace a line in the middle and write the words PATIENT SIDE on one side. Write or draw what you do to be patient on your patient side, and write or illustrate your other qualities on the other side. Think about skills, virtues, or what makes you unique. Cut out the shape and decorate.

Activity 2: 10 steps to patience

Think of how hard it is sometimes to be patient and how we need to learn patience to be able to accomplish a lot of things in life. Write down 10 steps that will help you learn to be patient. Steps could include looking within ourselves, remembering why patience is important, not looking at the clock, making a plan... You choose what steps help you. When you have written down your list of 10 steps, decorate it and share it with others.

NEED:
Colouring tools []
Writing tools []
Papers []

Step 10 Step 9 Step 8 Step 7 Step 6 Step 5 Step 4 Step 3 Step 2 Step 1

Put it somewhere or carry it with you where it will serve as a reminder to be patient.

Virtue Challenge: A ten step project.

Next time you feel like getting upset or yelling,
count back from 10, take a deep breath, and ask yourself:
what would I do if I was a little more patient? Then do that.

☐ ☐
WILL TRY   DONE

---

16. Respect

Understanding Respect:

Here are some words associated with Respect.

APPRECIATION   REVERENCE

ADMIRATION   CONSIDERATION   GRATITUDE

Using 2 of them, write your own definition of what Respect means to you.

_____

_____

OR

Write 2 sentences showing people practicing Respect using 1 suggested word in each sentence.

_____

_____

A beautiful quote about Respect:

Write down a quote that you wish
to memorize or remember.
If you cannot find a quote to inspire you,
try coming up with your own.

Activity 1: Programming respect

Discuss the use of television as a medium for communication and how it can be used as a tool to transmit different messages. Discuss what other media people use to send out information and messages. Share different shows you watch on television aimed at your age group and think about what kind of messages these show send.

Alone or in groups, pretend that you are a television producer in charge of creating a program that shows respect. What would this program be like? Think of the different ways we can show respect. Choose what your message is going to be and how you are going to transmit it. Discuss how we can all make an effort to spread more respect.

NEED:
Writing tools []
Papers []

Activity 2: Tree planting for someone

NEED:
A small plant, tree or seed []
Thick papers []
Gardening tools []
Eye-dropper []
Papers []
Straws []
Ink []

Discuss the impact of trees on our lives. Discuss the importance of respect when it comes to nature and our environment. Discuss the impact of tree planting in creating balance and the survival of our environment. Discuss how we show respect for the world when different people have different ideas of how we should live. As a group or individually, plant a tree as a gift for someone else. You can also plant one in memory of someone who has passed away. Using the paper and instructions below, make a card and give it to the person you have planted the tree for. If you plant something in someone's memory, write a card explaining who the tree is dedicated to and give the card to their family.

Instructions for the card:

Use the eye-dropper to place a few drops of ink at the bottom of your card.

Blow through the straw while the ink is still wet to make the ink move in different directions and look like a growing tree.

Virtue Challenge: Show respect.

Show respect for people.
Start saying **hello** to people you interact with
and look them in the eyes when you do.

WILL TRY   DONE

17. Responsibility

Understanding Responsibility:

Here are some words associated with Responsibility.

| DEPENDABLE | CARE |
| ACCOUNTABLE | RELIABLE | TRUSTWORTHY |

Using 2 of them, write your own definition of what Responsibility means to you.

_____

_____

OR

Write 2 sentences showing people practicing Responsibility using 1 suggested word in each sentence.

_____

_____

A beautiful quote about Responsibility: Write down a quote that you wish to memorize or remember. If you cannot find a quote to inspire you, try coming up with your own.

33

Activity 1: Responsible for the earth

Discuss your role and responsibility as someone living on the earth and using her land and resources. What is your responsibility toward future generations? What can you do to become more responsible in your own household and your immediate environment? Make a list of 10 steps you can carry out and find a partner who is willing to encourage you and help you become more responsible for your actions.
Get your family to help and make a plan.

NEED:
Writing tools []
Papers []

Here are some examples to get you started:
Recycle.
Make a list of disposable items you use around your house and think of alternatives.
Turn off unnecessary lights and encourage your family to use more efficient light bulbs.
Only run the dishwasher or washing machine with full loads.
Reduce what you consume.

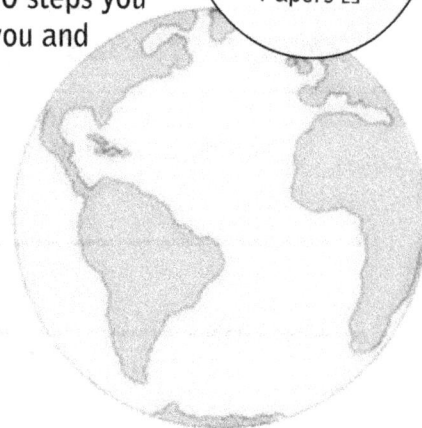

Activity 2: Responsible advertisement

NEED:
Papers []
Colouring tools []
Poster []
Large box []
Scissors []

Discuss what responsible advertising means. Share different advertisement you have seen recently and discuss whether or not you feel that responsibility was used when creating these advertisements. Pretend you are in charge of creating an advertisement to promote responsibility in advertising. Cut part of the box out to turn it into a television. Write your advertisement down and make sure you add your points about why responsibility in advertising is important. Use the poster and papers to create props for your presentation. Practice your advertisement before presenting it to others.
Discuss the importance of responsibility in advertising and media.

Virtue Challenge: A recycling project.

Does your school recycle? What about your family?
What can you do to start the process or increase
the amount being recycled?

WILL TRY   DONE

18. Self-awareness

Understanding Self-awareness:

Here are some words associated with Self-awareness.

CONSCIOUS   RESPONSIBLE

ATTENTIVE   KNOWLEDGE   MINDFUL

Using 2 of them, write your own definition of what Self-awareness means to you.

_____

_____

OR

Write 2 sentences showing people practicing Self-awareness using 1 suggested word in each sentence.

_____

_____

A beautiful quote about Self-awareness:

Write down a quote that you wish to memorize or remember.
If you cannot find a quote to inspire you, try coming up with your own.

Activity 1: High road, low road

Imagine two different roads. On one road you are called upon to do the right thing and to demonstrate the virtues and qualities that benefit everyone. On the other road you are encouraged to be selfish and do only things for your own benefit.

On a large piece of paper draw two roads, a high road and a low road. Write down three different scenarios or problems and how you would solve these problems using the high road and the low road. Examples of problems could be: Someone at school has been spreading a rumor about you and you just found. Your mom is always late in dropping you off but you are the one who gets in trouble. A friend is having some trouble at school and asks for your help. Draw these two roads on a sheet of paper and illustrate them as if they were actual roads. What traffic signs would you find on the side of the high road? On the low road? Use your imagination.

NEED:
Papers []
Colouring tools []
Writing tools []

Activity 2: Inside myself

NEED:

Large papers or posters []
Drawing tools []
Colouring tools []

I am LOVING

This activity is about self-expression and self-exploration. Discuss how in order to be assertive and to learn how to express ourselves we have to be aware of our own strengths and weaknesses. Lie down on a large paper and have someone else trace your outline. Once you have your outline, fill in the missing information. Fill in the virtues and qualities you have inside and add details to match the way you look like on the outside.

Try to relate your strengths and weaknesses to the physical area they may be associated with. For example, where the hands are you can write **creative** or **artistic**. Where the ears are you can write **good listener**. Share your drawing with others.

Virtue Challenge: A self-perception project.

Take a sheet of paper and in big letters write down 10 amazing things that you are going to accomplish during your lifetime.
At the bottom of the list write,
"I am full of possibilities. I can create great things when I allow my own gifts and abilities to shine." You can re-write the last sentence, but the meaning should be the same.

WILL TRY   DONE

19. Service

Understanding Service:

Here are some words associated with Service.

| ASSISTANCE | AID |
| HELP | SUPPORT | KINDNESS |

Using 2 of them, write your own definition of what Service means to you.

_____

_____

OR

Write 2 sentences showing people practicing Service using 1 suggested word in each sentence.

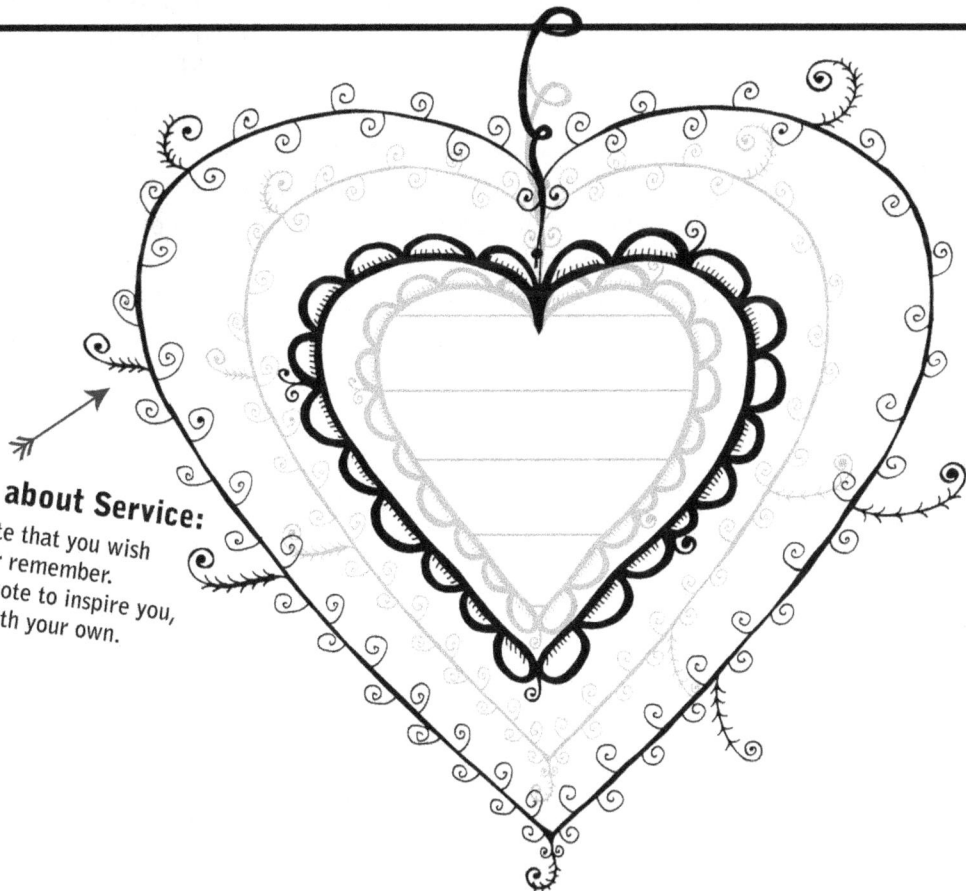

_____

_____

A beautiful quote about Service:
Write down a quote that you wish to memorize or remember. If you cannot find a quote to inspire you, try coming up with your own.

Activity 1: Making a difference

If you think you are too small to make a difference, try sleeping in a room with a mosquito.
– African proverb

What do you think this proverb means? How would you relate the proverb to service? Can you find other quotes that are more inspiring? Come up with your own service project. Here are some guidelines to make it more inspirational and challenging. Sit down and come up with ideas for your service project. Follow through with your ideas!

-Involve your family or friends.
-Give yourself a name, logo and mission - a mission can be one sentence that narrows down what kind of service you want your group to be involved in.
-Decide how much time you are willing to give.
-Do some research about the needs in your community or neighborhood.
-Inspire yourself from a personal hero.
-Think big.
-Give yourself a challenge.
-Make a commitment and stick to it!
-Find other quotes and sayings that inspire you to action.
-Have fun!

Activity 2: Create a service tree

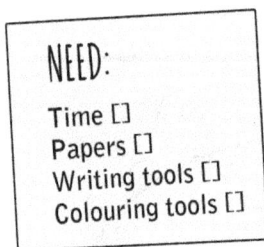

A telephone tree is a system in which each person will call another and so on in case of an emergency or when people want to share news. Using the same principle, create a service tree. Fold your paper in half to make a nice, big card. On the front draw a service tree and write down what your service tree will be about. You can choose a theme of service or leave it up to each person to choose their own type of service. Inside the card write your name and next to that write the name of someone you are going to help out. Think of something you can do for them and when you have done it, pass on your card to the next person asking them to continue the service tree. Follow up and see how far it goes. Try starting a few service trees.

Virtue Challenge: Think about these words.

Only a life lived in the service to others is worth living.   - Albert Einstein

Do you agree?

WILL TRY   DONE

---

20. Trust

Understanding Trust:

Here are some words associated with Trust.

| BELIEVE | RELY ON |

| COUNT ON | CONFIDENCE | TRUTH |

Using 2 of them, write your own definition of what Trust means to you.

_____

_____

OR

Write 2 sentences showing people practicing Trust using 1 suggested word in each sentence.

_____

_____

A beautiful quote about Trust:

Write down a quote that you wish
to memorize or remember.
If you cannot find a quote to inspire you,
try coming up with your own.

Activity 1: Holding the remote

Pretend that you are holding a remote that affects the behaviour of the people around you. You are being entrusted with choosing how people behave and this is a great responsibility. Create a large remote with different buttons on it. Have each button affect someone's behaviour. Think about buttons for changing the channel, turning the volume up or down, muting, pressing rewind or fast forward, pressing stop, as well as others you may want to invent. When you are holding the remote, you get to tell others what to do as if they were on television. Give everyone a chance to hold the remote.

Discuss what it feels like to have to trust someone else or have others trust you. Talk about power and responsibility in relation to trust.

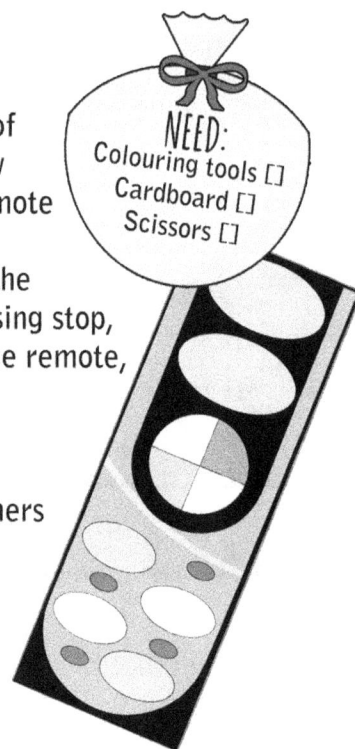

NEED:
Colouring tools []
Cardboard []
Scissors []

Activity 2: You can trust me

NEED:

Drawing tools []
Writing tools []
Papers []

Look at the list below and circle the answers that show good reasons to be considered trustworthy. When you are done, make a list of 10 reasons why you should be trusted. Make yourself a small card to keep as a reminder and place it somewhere where you can see it easily. Share your list or your card with someone you trust.

I TRY TO ALWAYS BE ON TIME.
I MAY BE LATE, BUT I AM THE LIFE OF THE PARTY.
I SOMETIMES KEEP MY WORD, WHEN IT'S NOT TOO HARD.
I ALWAYS DO WHAT I SAY.
I KEEP MOST OF MY PROMISES, MOST OF THE TIME.
I OFTEN TELL THE TRUTH.
I AM RESPONSIBLE WITH OTHER PEOPLE'S MONEY.
I LOST MY FRIEND'S CAP WHEN I BORROWED IT, BUT IT WASN'T THAT NICE.
I KNOW HOW TO COOK.
I PUT THINGS BACK AFTER I AM DONE WITH THEM.

Virtue Challenge: Can you be trusted?

Ask yourself these questions:
Can my friends trust me? Can my family trust me?
Do I keep my word? Do I do what I say I will? Am I often late and unreliable?

Based on your answers, ask yourself:
What can I do to be more trustworthy?

WILL TRY   DONE

41

Scenario	Person A	Person B	Person C
Person A has just stolen a loaf of bread and person B is watching but does not say anything.			
Person A, B and C are standing in front of the food bank			
Person B and C were talking and B suddenly starts to cry			
Person A is standing in a hospital waiting room			
Person B is yelling at person C			

English	Hello	Goodbye	Thank you	Can I help?
Mandarin	Nǐ hǎo	Zàijiàn	Xièxiè	Wǒ shìfǒu néng bāngzhù?
French	Bonjour	Au revoir	Merci	Je peux vous aider?
Arabic	As-salām 'alaykum	Ma'a as-salāmah	Shukraan	Hal yumkinuni almusaeadat
Inuktikut	Ai'	Tavvaujutit	Qujannamiik	Ikajurunnaqpunga?
Spanish				
Hindu				
Dutch				
Swahili				

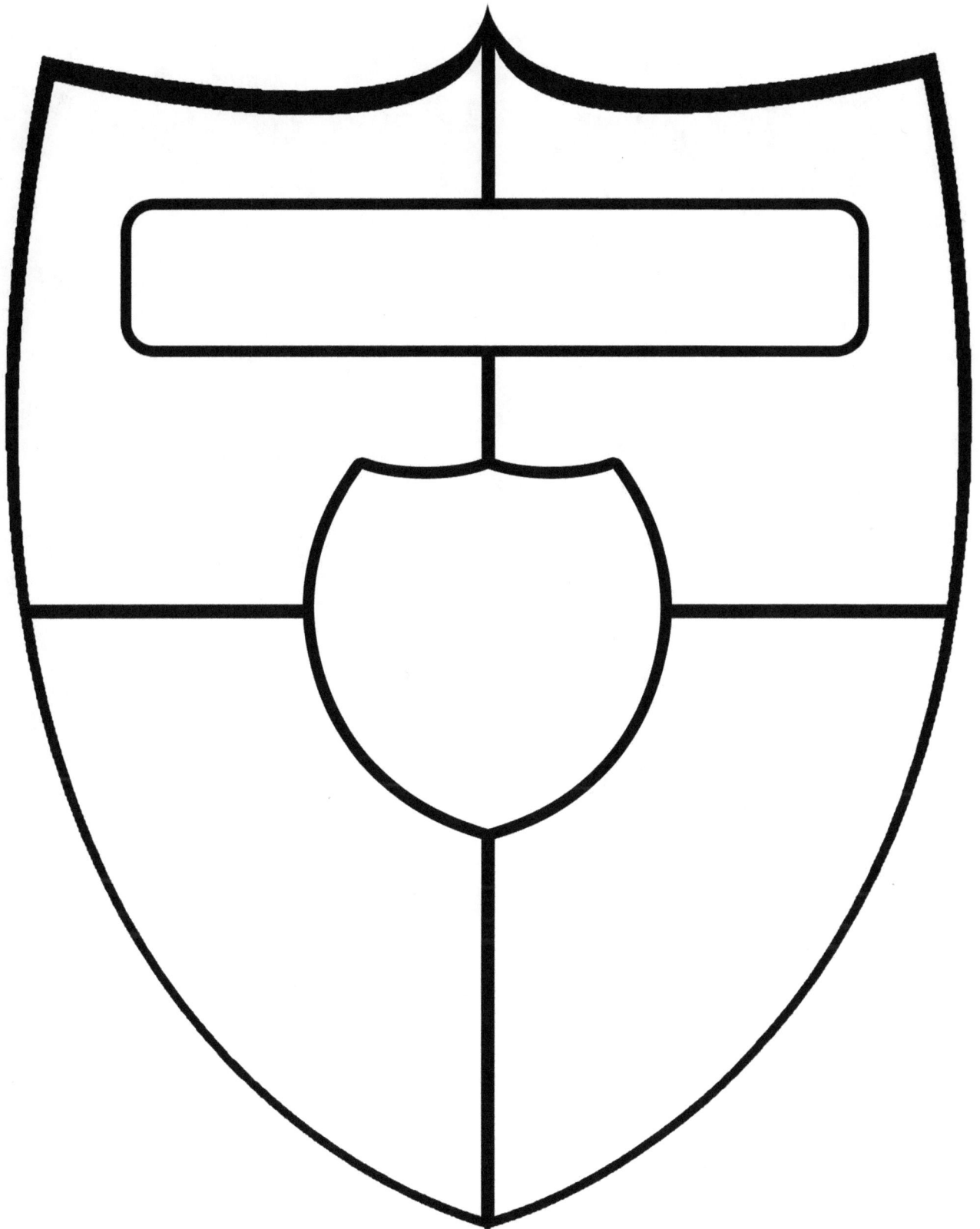

47